THE HEART AND SOUL OF SAFETY

LEADING SAFETY PERFORMANCE FROM THE HEART

PAUL ESPENAN

Published by Freiling Agency, LLC.

P.O. Box 1264
Warrenton, VA 20188

www.FreilingAgency.com

PB ISBN: 978-1-969826-17-7
HB ISBN: 978-1-969826-18-4
E-book ISBN: 978-1-969826-19-1

God wastes nothing.

CONTENTS

PREFACE

My dad and his partners ran an occupational medicine clinic. Some of my earliest memories are stories that Dad would tell at the dinner table as he described his day. He often told stories about how he had stitched up someone's hand from a work injury, perhaps at a restaurant or even someone who had caught their hand in a box-stapler machine.

When I was old enough, I began working at the clinic and observed patients with their various work-related injuries, sometimes watching him stitch up someone. I'm certain that my dad's love and care for his patients had a very profound influence on me that ultimately led me to a love of safety and incident prevention. My professional route to safety and everything related to safety was not as direct as it could have been, but when it arrived, it was abundantly clear it was my calling. I was drawn to the principle that all incidents can be prevented and became passionately curious about motivational theory. My research and observations on how incidents are prevented led me again and again to pure leadership instruction and action as the antidote. Why not promote safety leadership as opposed to just plain leadership? My response has always been, "It's the same thing!"

I admire what Paul O'Neill did at Alcoa. He made safety and good business practices synonymous. Leadership and accountability are forever tied to safety performance. If you show me a well-run company, I'll show you a safe one (and vice versa too!).

THIS BOOK

Through many years of leading Environmental, Health, and Safety efforts for large organizations, I discovered that everyone needs constant inspiration. For companies to stay engaged in safety culture, there must be a fuel that feeds the desire to be safe and sustains this focus with passion in front of our distracted brains. In 2020, I began delivering safety leadership moments for my organization's operations conference calls. No one had asked me to do this, it just seemed right. My goal was to inspire leaders to take ownership of safety, make it uniquely their own, and most importantly to act. Beyond that idea, I had no specific strategy for where this effort might go, how I would sustain it, or for that matter how well-received it would be. The answer to those questions began to trickle in over the weeks as various members of our leadership team would provide feedback, all very positive, and some of it quite emotional. That positive feedback was all I needed to continue. One day my boss asked me, "When are you going to write a book?" The rest is history.

This book is not intended to be read from cover to cover. It is designed to be read as one segment per week as a foundation to craft your own safety leadership moments. To be effective, I recommend you customize the message and make it yours. We've left room for that. There may be some moments you want to share "as-is" but you'll gain much more if you customize it and add your own flavor. The result will be a boost to your authenticity, a very necessary ingredient for your own leadership.

1

COMPLACENT

"Success breeds complacency. Complacency breeds failure.
Only the paranoid survive."
—Andy Grove

"I think it's dangerous to think that you're successful,
because then you become complacent."
—Tommy Hilfiger

The summer between my freshman and sophomore year in college, I was on Lake Pontchartrain near New Orleans with my older brother and a few of his friends. A thunderstorm rolled in and we beached the boat at an abandoned amusement park on the shores of the lake. After the rain stopped, we returned. Rainwater had accumulated in the boat. My brother instructed me to pull the plug from the rear transom to allow the water to flow out. As I was doing this, standing in water with my hand in the water, lightning struck me. A jolt of electricity ripped through me. It was unlike anything I had ever felt before. As I fell to the floor of the boat, my heart skipped a few beats before continuing. With incredulous shock on their faces, everyone was exclaiming things. "Damn that was close... it hit you, it hit you!" At the time, dazed and unaware, I didn't grasp what had just happened. Later that day, when I got home, I reflected on the greater meaning—I felt an undeniable pull—a sign that God was urging me to change my path, with good reason. But, I soon rejected that notion and returned to my old way of life. Complacency crept in.

I once did a survey in a large group of several hundred people. I asked for a show of hands how many people had ever had a very close call while driving, an incident that could have easily killed them. Had they ever said, "Damn that was close, that could have killed us!" At least half of the group raised their hands. I then asked, "What changed after that event?" Silence. Maybe things changed for a short time, but they soon returned to the old ways.

It's madness that we can receive such clear safety messages, sometimes about our path in life or about our personal safety, then ignore them. I managed to ignore the lightning strike. The same thing has likely happened to you.

The job of a safety leader is to receive the safety messages that come in many forms (hopefully it does not take a lightning strike) and do all things necessary to change safety for the better. If we are not agents for change, we will just get the unacceptable default unsafe future. We must recognize the signs and take action. We cannot allow complacency to sneak back in.

How does the feeling of being safe allow complacency to slowly creep in?

What role do positive safety habits play in keeping complacency in check?

2

RAINBOW

*"Daydream. Because you can't accomplish
what you've never fully imagined."*
—Richelle E. Goodrich

*"The future belongs to those who believe
in the beauty of their dreams."*
—Eleanor Roosevelt

Perhaps you've heard the expression "pay no attention to the man behind the curtain." For this story, please do pay attention. Lyman Frank Baum was the seventh of nine children, and he became a daydreamer who got little attention from his parents. When he was twelve, he spent two years at a military academy, but after being severely disciplined for daydreaming, he likely had a psychogenic heart attack. His weak heart kept him inside, so he spent many days dreaming of fantasy lands where "somewhere over the rainbow" he would find a pot of gold.

By the age of thirty, he had tried to be a journalist, a printer, postage stamp dealer, poultry breeder, and trade journal publisher, all of which failed. He started his own theater, becoming his own writer, director, and lead actor. Most of his plays were not successful, and his theater failed. He married despite his future mother-in-law's warnings that he was not mentally present. He and his bride moved to the Dakota Territory and opened an emporium specializing in Bohemian glass, paper lanterns, and gourmet chocolates. They went bankrupt. They moved to Chicago and his mother-in-law watched him captivate his children with magical stories. She suggested he write children's books, which he did.

His second book was a novel for children, and while searching for a title he noted the label on the bottom drawer of a file cabinet "O-Z." He had his title.

Every publishing company turned him down until one offered to print it if he paid the cost himself. He waited until the first copies were sold. During Christmas of 1900, he could not afford to buy presents for his children, so in desperation he went to the publishing company in hopes of finding a royalty check. He could not look at it, so he took it home to his wife who nearly fainted when she saw the amount. It was $1,423— or about $45,000 dollars in today's dollars.

Lyman passed away in 1919, so he never saw what became of his book that became a movie in 1939, *The Wonderful Wizard of OZ*. He did not live to see his creation become etched on our minds so much that even a cryptic reference to "paying attention to the man behind the curtain" has become part of our vernacular.

What this proves is that God does not waste anything, there are no wasted moments. The darkest storms make the brightest rainbows. We always have hope and "hope does not disappoint"—as Paul said in his letter to the Romans (5:5).

No matter the natural disaster, or the challenge of our day or week, or whatever personal junk we carry around, we always have hope. If we find our minds wandering during our day, taking our attention from our work or distracting us from focusing on safely performing the task in front of us, two things come to mind. 1) Nothing is wasted, especially in safety. When things go wrong, we must see the opportunity to learn and grow. 2) Daydreams might produce something amazing like they did for Lyman Frank Baum, but no matter the weight of our problems, in the midst of our distractions we can regain our focus because we always have hope, somewhere over the rainbow.

In our distracted world, how many incidents occur due to distractions?

How can our daily distractions become an opportunity to improve our safety focus?

3

—

COOL

"Tell me and I forget, teach me and I may remember, involve me and I learn."
—Benjamin Franklin

"Training is not an expense, but an investment in human capital."
—Roy H. Williams

Neil Armstrong is famously known as being the first man to walk on the moon, but his life tells a greater story for us if we look at the life events that led to his being the person who was given this opportunity.

In the movie *First Man*, we learn a great deal about Armstrong's personal life, marriage, and hardship. One event stands out. During Gemini 8, in March of 1966, Armstrong and pilot David Scott successfully performed the first docking of two spacecraft. Soon after, a stuck thruster caused the joined spacecraft to roll so much that it would have been fatal, but Armstrong managed to stay cool and conscious and use re-entry fuel to stabilize the roll. By all accounts the mission should have resulted in their death. By staying cool, they managed to stay alive. Scott later said, "The guy was brilliant. He knew the system so well. He found the solution, he activated the solution, under extreme circumstances ... it was my lucky day to be flying with him." (See the Smithsonian Channel video about the crisis; it is also depicted in the Neil Armstrong biopic *First Man*.)

Every day we make safety decisions that depend on our innate ability to get things right, including our ability to be lucky, sometimes under extreme circumstances. Many of our good catches would be serious incidents, but for good luck. Even with increases in automation we still have to think about safety and what we would do in the event of an emergency. Quick thinking and training are the building blocks to create this firm foundation that we depend on to be safe.

As leaders, our challenge is to give our full and enthusiastic support of performing the required training, making it meaningful, and making it applicable and real, to provide the foundation for when things go wrong.

How do you view training? Is it a burden or an opportunity?

Name a time in your life when training and experience made all the difference.

4

LEGACY

*"Legacy. What is a legacy? It's planting seeds
in the garden you won't get to see."*
—From *Hamilton, the Musical*

"To live in hearts we leave behind is not to die."
—Thomas Campbell

Swedeborg, Missouri, had an opportunity to name their elementary school building, and everyone knew it had to be very thoughtful and deliberate. According to the kids, it had to be someone you just knew would be right. Tradition is to name schools after such people like George Washington, Abraham Lincoln, or even famous people from the State. With this abundance of people from history, Swedeborg, Missouri, went with Claudine Wilson.

And who exactly was Claudine you ask? That would be the school custodian or janitor. The kids described her as focused, dedicated, and in the zone. Over the past thirty years she had taken on a number of added responsibilities like bus driver, lunch duty, groundskeeping, repairs, and even phone operator. Her only motivation was the kids, who she says "have your heart." Everyone knows that when a kid is sick or troubled, they go see Claudine. And the school board voted unanimously to name the building after her. There was just one person who did not agree: Claudine. In the end, though, the kids said they would want to be like her.

Claudine is a perfect example that titles mean nothing when it comes to leading. Everyone leads from where they are. You can be the janitor and still change lives! Our influence will be our legacy, whether there are buildings named after us or not. As leaders, our challenge comes down to answering this question: what will our legacy be? What will our safety legacy be? If you don't like what your legacy already is, do something different starting today.

How can we change behaviors in a positive way by focusing on our legacy?

Imagine your own funeral where your eulogy is given, what words do you want to hear?

5

RACKET

"Ninety-nine percent of the failures come from people who have the habit of making excuses."
—George Washington Carver

"All your excuses are lies."
—Jocko Willink

During the Prohibition Era, a fake storefront would be put up to fool the authorities. Alcohol would be sold out of the back, and the storefront would make the operation look legit. The larger operation was called a "racket," the source of the word racketeering, meaning dishonest dealing.

In modern business, a "racket" is defined as a constant complaint plus a fixed way of being. The constant complaint becomes a fixture, a construct, something fake, something made up, just like a storefront during prohibition. When something fails, we can blame the racket and go back to our work, dismissing the idea that we can make a difference. The problem with this convenient excuse is that in most cases it's fake and just an empty facade. It might sound like this:

- The reason that safety incidents happen is because leadership does not care.

- Why should I try to fix this? It will just end up back this way.
- Why should I say anything? No one will listen.

All of this is simply a lack of ownership. Such defeatism can easily become a racket.

When it comes to safety we are always working for our loved ones, or our "home team." We can have all the pride in the world for the company's way of life or the brand, but in the end it won't matter who we worked for, but it will matter if we did it safely. There can be no excuses for not owning it for the sake of the home team, if for nothing else. If you see defeatism in those you lead, you need to nip it powerfully in the bud. It's like cancer and it will grow. Our jobs as leaders are to remove the cancer of defeatism.

What are some of the excuses you have heard for not working safe?

What happens if we don't respond to those excuses?

6

ADVERSITY

*"The most successful people see adversity not as
a stumbling block, but as a stepping-stone to greatness."*
—Shawn Achor

*"Fire is the test of gold;
adversity, of strong men."*
—Seneca

We know about Post Traumatic Stress Disorder or PTSD—
when the stress and trauma of the battlefield persist off
the battlefield as if the war was still being fought. But have you
heard of post traumatic growth?

Post traumatic growth holds that people who endure psychological struggle following adversity can often see positive growth afterward. The main difference in predicting outcomes is one factor: the people who say, "Woe is me," versus the people who ask themselves, "What will I make of this?"

When we find greater meaning in our struggles, we increase the likelihood we will benefit and grow from the experience.

There are days when being safe is hard: immediately after a traumatic event, when our mental strength is failing, when our personal junk of life encroaches into our work, and we use all we are to just keep going, let alone be at our best. Safety is easier when things are going well.

When it comes to safety, and incidents occur, it's traumatic to everyone around it: the injured, the coworker, the larger team, and even the safety professional. In the aftermath, a decision is presented: will we fail forward or feel sorry for ourselves?

The importance of practicing and making a habit of positive self-talk cannot be overstated. What we tell ourselves matters greatly, and it determines the outcome more than we know. Faking it until we make it turns into success. As leaders our challenge is to ask ourselves and those we influence: "What will we make of this?"

I recently spent time with a team that had made two years safe. I noticed how they acted with the belief that they would be successful. It is that same level of belief in our moment of depression that will make us safe. Not false confidence, but confidence that we are making safe choices, not operating on luck.

$\Longleftarrow$

Do you look at incidents as opportunities or setbacks?

Do you know people who have overcome adversity by finding meaning and telling a greater story?

7

RESILIENCE

*"To share your weakness is to make yourself vulnerable;
to make yourself vulnerable is to show your strength."*
—Crissi Jami

*"Vulnerability is not winning or losing.
It's having the courage to show up when you can't
control the outcome."*
—Brene Brown

Recent research on the neuroscience of motivation and persistence supports theories about why some people quit and others retain the brainpower to keep working persistently. The research helps us understand why it is difficult for both world-class athletes and everyday people to sustain their motivation and persistence. The fMRI-based research shows that two types of fatigue (recoverable vs unrecoverable) activate specific parts of the frontal cortex (the part of the brain that is required to be able to focus and work safely). Recoverable fatigue appears to benefit from our brain's assessing that a reward's value is worth the sustained effort. New research (Müller et al., 2021) into the neural mechanisms of perseverance suggests that two types of effort-based fatigue can reduce someone's willingness to exert effort for reward; the first short-term type of fatigue is "recoverable" after a break, whereas the second, longer-term type of fatigue is "unrecoverable." This underscores the importance of resilience and recharging to allow mental recovery.

Fatigue must be recognized as part of human nature but also for the hazard it can become. We all need motivation and reasons to keep trying. Through a greater understanding of ourselves, we can recognize when our head is not in the game or see the signs that others have checked out. If we don't have the psychological safety zone of being able to honestly admit our fatigue, we run the risk of continuing in this vulnerable "unrecoverable" fatigued state. Safety leaders must create mental safety zones, where anything can be shared with the certainty that it will be placed in the best possible context. It is only with this vulnerability that we will be able to talk about ALL of the hazards that exist and how we can properly mitigate them.

What are you doing to create psychological safety zones in your organization?

Does your culture support vulnerability and honesty?

8

GROWTH

*"Don't it always seem to go, that you don't know what
you've got till it's gone. They paved paradise
and put up a parking lot."*
—from the song "Big Yellow Taxi" by Joni Mitchell

*"Be not afraid of growing slowly;
be afraid only of standing still."*
—Chinese Proverb

We grow in height until the ages of about fifteen and twenty-one. We grow in many ways as leaders, but unfortunately, we may stop growing at a very early age. Sometimes we may find a person committed to a personal growth plan into their thirties, forties, or beyond. Many people stop investing in themselves.

As John Maxwell teaches us:

"Leaders never get to the point where their influence has maxed out; they always have unreached potential waiting to be fulfilled. In leadership, how far you go depends on how much you grow. Unlike your physical height, your growth as a leader is within your control; you can do something about it."

To be effective, safety must be deliberate and intentional. Safety never ends.

If we don't focus on the specific task of growing safety, we won't grow.

If we are not aware of our safety strengths and shortcomings, we won't grow.

If we don't make a consistent and disciplined investment in our safety growth, we won't grow.

We can go halfway on safety efforts and stop, coast, or neglect our safety growth. When this happens the likelihood of incidents increases. We must continue to make the effort in the right ways if we expect positive results.

In what ways have we taken safety performance for granted?

What are the consequences of a safety culture that stops growing?

9

FAVOR

If you can't return a favor, pass it on."
—Louise Brown

"To accept a favor from a friend is to confer one."
—John Churton Collins

Would you please do a favor for me? Have you noticed that when we are asked to do a favor by a coworker, a friend, a family member, immediately the possibility of help comes to the front of our brains and hearts. So, today, as a friend, I am asking you this favor. Would you please ask all you lead or influence to do a favor for you? Ask them as friends to "please do their best to work safely today." And when they have completed this task, ask them to please let you know that they have done it.

Why? When we remove all constructs of title, position, or stature down to the friendship level, we are all just human. One human to another, a request for a simple favor is hard to resist and quite powerful.

Are you leading with the power of friendship?

What favors should you be asking of those you lead?

10

ROOM

"Always leave room for the unexpected.
A buffer of time, a little extra money, a reserve of goodwill.
You won't be maximizing every opportunity or squeezing out
every last dollar, but what you lose in reward,
you gain in safety. Survival is the highest return of all."
—James Clear

"Keep some room in your heart for the unimaginable."
—Mary Oliver

It doesn't matter if you order coffee or make it in the automatic machines at a truck stop. The baristas or the button on the machine both ask for a choice: leave room for cream?

I grew up in New Orleans where babies are weaned on café au lait, which translates from French as "coffee with milk." It's no surprise that I have a little coffee with my cream. For me cream is the best part.

Do we leave room in our lives for cream: the good stuff? Or is our black coffee a metaphor for our life or even our workday?

Safety is the good stuff!

If we don't see safety as the best part, we might not leave room for it! As leaders, the question becomes: do we view safety as the best part—as something we must make room for?

What changes do you need to make in your leadership so that safety is the good stuff?

What excitement can you add to make safety the good stuff?

11

TODOY

"Yesterday's the past, tomorrow's the future,
but today is a gift. That's why it's called the present."
—Bil Keane

"Today is a new day. Even if you were wrong yesterday,
you can get it right today."
—Dwight Howard

The 2019 Washington Nationals season has some safety lessons for us. After fifty games, they were nineteen and thirty-one and were given a 0.1 percent chance of winning the pennant, and only a 3.8 percent chance of even getting in the playoffs. Coach Dave Martinez came up with a motto, "Be one and "O" today." And the team did just that the rest of the year and... they won the World Series!

Winning is about the present and turning the smallest victories into big ones by simply repeating them. When we do simple better, we can win. In the *Meet the Parents* movie, Ben Stiller was asked to say a prayer and he did not know what to say. He wasn't a praying man, so he had no idea what to say. Then without thinking he begins to say the lyrics to the song "Day by Day" from Godspell. Day by Day. Simple but effective.

The only way we can be present to our work and be where our boots are is by focusing on today, the here and now. As safety leaders, we need to be one and "O" today, then do that 365 times a year. Infuse this simple idea to those you lead, especially when the worries and distractions of the world come.

What requests can you make of those you lead that will help them make one safe day?

What are the chances of having a safe year versus having a safe day?

12

SILLY

"We are all a little weird and life's a little weird, and when we find someone whose weirdness is compatible with ours, we join up with them and fall in mutual weirdness and call it love."
—Dr. Seuss

"To be yourself in a world that is constantly trying to make you something else is the greatest accomplishment."
—Ralph Waldo Emerson

Wilt Chamberlain played professional basketball from 1959 to 1973. He set multiple NBA records but was also known for being a terrible free-throw shooter. His career average was 51 percent. In the 1961-1962 season, Chamberlain made a change to try to improve his free-throw percentage. He adopted the style employed by the best free-throw shooter at that time, Rick Barry. "The granny shot," where he held the ball between his legs and shot it underhand. Rick Barry's career free-throw percentage was a remarkable 89 percent. Barry later explained why he chose to shoot that way, mentioning it was a more natural motion with less things to go wrong. While experimenting with Barry's method, on March 2, 1962, Chamberlain scored 100 points in an NBA game, making twenty-eight of thirty free throws. This record still holds! Despite his success, Chamberlain gave up on the granny shot. Chamberlain said this about the granny shot in his autobiography: "I felt silly, like a sissy, shooting underhanded. I know I was wrong. I know some of the best foul shooters in history shot that way. Even now the best one in the NBA, Rick Barry, shoots underhanded. I just couldn't do it."

I'm certain you can relate. Rick Barry didn't care what people thought about him and shot in a way that others ridiculed. Wilt Chamberlain allowed what others wrongly thought to influence his good decision that had achieved fantastic results.

As leaders, we must first be our authentic selves. Without authenticity we won't build trust. Secondly, while appearances might matter in business settings, so do good results and safe days. When it comes to safety, we cannot be concerned about ridicule or what others might say. We have to embrace safety no matter the circumstances, even when it seems awkward or looks funny. There is no room for peer pressure when being safe, there is only room for integrity. Lastly, a positive safety culture always supports the safe choice, no matter how it looks.

~

Describe a time when being safe felt awkward.

When safety belts were first introduced it felt awkward. Now, not wearing safety belts feels awkward. How does changing safety practices make people feel awkward?

13

ENCOURAGE

"Correction does much,
but encouragement does more."
—Johann Wolfgang von Goethe

"Be an encourager, the world has plenty
of critics already."
—Dave Willis

A thirty-seven-year-old man living in a small West Virginia town washed cars for a living. As he worked, he sang. Others heard him singing and encouraged him to try out one of the talent contests on television. Eventually he did just that. He won the *America's Got Talent* competition.

We've all heard the salutation "Take Care." But what does that really mean? It means to be your own best friend. Be kind to yourself. Eat right, sleep well, take time for yourself, and get an annual physical just to be sure. That's encouragement. Landau Eugene Murphy Jr. was encouraged to invest in himself, and the results were amazing. He signed with a major recording company. All of us need this kind of encouragement, especially if we are going to be there for others.

It's a powerful safety reminder to "be where your boots are." It's a call to mindfulness. But before we can reflect on being mindful, we need to actually "be" first.

As safety leaders, our challenge is to receive encouragement from others, then spread encouragement to all who we influence so they will do the same. Every day, we can tell those who we influence that we believe in them. The results will be a stronger foundation on which to build our safety efforts.

Who believes in you and encourages you?

Describe a time when a small amount of encouragement made a difference for you.

14

TEST

*"It's 44 degrees and it's nice and rainy outside.
But no one cares about that. It's not about the rain,
it's what the rain represents. Life is always giving you a test,
trying to give you a way out."*
—David Goggins

*"Courage is not simply one of the virtues,
but the form of every virtue at the testing point."*
—C.S. Lewis

As I started up the truck early on the fourth day, the gravelly voiced female radio host said, "I know many of you are going through challenging times." An obvious reference to the recent floods in southern Louisiana that had devastated thousands of homes. I was bone-tired after three very long days of tearing out the wet wallboard and carpet from my sister's house. The radio announcer continued, "But there is no testimony without a test." How true. It is certainly during the times of struggle that we create our testimony. How will we respond when the trials come? Will we recognize the trials as the benevolence of our higher power helping to form us?

Every one of us will face many tests each day. To be clear: everything in life is a test, a test to gauge our perseverance and determination.

Safety takes perseverance and determination. No matter what the challenge, we must remain ready. Others are watching how we lead, how we behave, looking for cues, especially when things aren't going well. If we relent in our pursuit of the prize (no incidents), or our personal adherence to the policies, procedures, and safe work practices, others can take those cues and relax. And that relaxation could lead to an incident.

Accept and own every test, especially the safety tests.

How can we transform our thinking so that we see and respond to the many tests that fill our day?

How can we adapt the "everything is a test" mindset?

15

EMPATHY

"Empathy is more powerful than sympathy."
—Angie Thomas

"The highest form of knowledge is empathy."
—Bill Bullard

In 1912, a man started conducting public speaking night classes and business education classes at the YMCA. Because he could not find any satisfactory handbook already in publication, he originally began writing small booklets to go along with his courses. After one of his fourteen-week courses, the man was approached by a publisher, who could not persuade him to publish his materials as a book. The publisher hired a stenographer to type up what he heard in one of the long lectures offered and presented the transcript to the man, which was edited and became the first edition.

Perhaps the most timeless and fundamental book on leadership principles, *How to Win Friends and Influence People* by Dale Carnegie was first published in 1936 and has sold over 30 million copies. The principles contained in this book should be incorporated into our success formulas. Here is just one example to illustrate one of Carnegie's points in winning people to your way of thinking:

"Try honestly to see things from the other person's point of view."

In short, be empathetic. If we don't understand the context and challenges of others, we are in no position to help them be successful or safe. Empathetic leaders will see things that others overlook, gaining important context. All conflict comes from a lack of shared context. Alignment of goals comes from shared context.

What is the role of empathy in being an effective safety leader?

What questions can we ask others to learn about their challenges?

16

ASSIST

Everyone can be great, because everyone can serve."
—Martin Luther King

"No one has ever become poor by giving."
—Anne Frank

John Stockton spent his entire NBA career as a point guard for the Utah Jazz, and the team made the playoffs in each of his nineteen seasons. Nobody thought that he was going to be this good. Nobody. But the thing was, nobody measured his heart. He leads the NBA's list of assists with 15,806! John's autobiography, *Assisted*, pulls back the curtain on his very personal life to show fans a thoughtful recounting of the people, places, and events that have connected with him along his path of extraordinary success. This book clearly illustrates the importance of his family, his faith, and his unparalleled competitive spirit. He talks about people like his grade school coach and college athletic trainer, and shares how, even to this day, the game of basketball continues to teach him life lessons.

I once made a list of all the people who have assisted me along my path. I then carved out some time to try to reach them and thank them for their investment. The list was long. I was overwhelmed with gratitude. They were beyond grateful for knowing they made a difference.

Dr. Kevin Elko often asks us, "Who can we bless today?" And I would ask you who can you assist today? When it comes to being safe, it takes many assists. That can take the form of a simple reminder, an encouraging word, or a challenge to stay focused and be successful. When we make the safety playoffs, it will be because of the many assists we've received. Who are you assisting to be safe?

How can we live the adage that a rising tide floats all boats?

Why are "assists" so important when it comes to safety?

17

JUST

"Pride makes us artificial,
and humility makes us real."
—Thomas Merton

"The greatest lesson in life is to know
that even fools are right sometimes."
—Winston Churchill

The other day, when a group was introducing themselves to one another, a person started to introduce themself with "I'm just..." I hear this quite a bit. My response is usually the same. There isn't anyone that is "just" anything. There are many parts to the body, but we are one body (company). And in that same spirit, every one of us plays a valuable role that is important to our success. Don't rob yourself or diminish yourself or kid yourself. You matter. The follow-up response I often receive is usually a conversation about humility and how they thought that "just" was part of being humble. A quote by C.S. Lewis that has really helped me understand humility is this: "Humility is not thinking less of yourself, it is thinking of yourself less." In other words, doing the very important work of being people for others.

When we talk about the importance of our work, we must connect to our higher purpose. Connecting to purpose is what will keep us connected and working together on our team.

As leaders it's not only important that we lead with humility, but also with clear purpose. Our purpose will influence others. As safety leaders, our purpose is to get as many people home safe as we can. We must think of others and be people for others so they can make it home safely. My challenge to all of you is to lead with true humility and purpose.

How can excessive pride become a barrier to being safe?

How does humility cause us to think of other's safety and well-being?

18

MOM

*"As I grow older, I pay less attention to what men say.
I just watch what they do."*
—Andrew Carnegie

*"Do not complain about growing old.
It is a privilege denied to many."*
—Mark Twain

Mother's Day is coming so please accept this as a heads up reminder to plan something. At the time of this writing, my mom is ninety-three, so I am not sure how many more Mother's Days I'll have with her on this earth.

Are leaders naturally born or do they learn to lead as they rise to the occasion? Either way, it's safe to say a mother has a hand in the development of leaders. Abraham Lincoln said, "All that I am, or hope to be, I owe to my angel mother." If you think about it, mothers teach us many principles of leadership, by perhaps, most importantly, giving guidance through failures and teaching. Add to that the important characteristics of self-confidence, decision making, problem solving, and even teamwork (getting along with friends), and you can see the importance of the influence of our mothers, or others who filled that same role.

I believe the answer to most of our challenges, especially safety, has everything to do with pure leadership: actions taken or not taken. The fact that we have made it this far (through the assistance of our mothers) is proof that we can go further still and that we should not and cannot rest, especially in our efforts to be safe. Our safe actions so far must continue all our days, especially those safe actions learned through our parents.

What is a safety lesson that you learned as a child? Why do you still remember it?

Why do adults violate safety principles that children know so well?

Has a child ever reminded you to be safe?

19

FIGHT

*"It is the duty of the good shepherd
to shear his sheep, not skin them."*
—Tiberius

*"Alone we can do so little;
together we can do so much."*
—Helen Keller

As we drove through northwestern Colorado, my coworker, who was driving, said, "If we take this dirt road we can save about twenty minutes, but sometimes you have to stop for the shepherds. This is sheep country and if the sheep are being moved, they will block the road, and we will have to wait." As we drove, sure enough, the road was blocked by thousands of sheep. I noticed that some of the "sheep" were actually very large dogs. These large dogs didn't herd the flock, they guarded it.

The Great Pyrenees or Pyrenean Mountain Dog is a large white livestock-guarding dog that tops out at 130 lbs. This dog is aggressive to any predator that may harm its flock. The dog stays with the sheep and looks a lot like a sheep, but predators soon learn that these sheep fight back. Then the predator thinks that all the sheep fight back. It's a great deterrent.

As leaders, are we fighting for those we lead when the predators arrive? Or do we leave it to chance? If we are defending from the predators, or "the enemies of being safe," we need to be actively pushing back everything that can harm our flock. Are we actively searching for ways to protect, looking for hazards or people that may harm them? We need to be fully engaged in what they are doing so we can know how to protect them in the first place.

What safety battles have you fought recently?

How is seeing safety hazards as predators helpful to our safety motivation?

20

SAMARITAN

"It takes many good deeds to build a good reputation,
and only one bad one to lose it."
—Benjamin Franklin

"Your brand is what people say about you
when you're not in the room."
—Jeff Bezos

When he was sixteen, Thomas Weller was driving on a snowy Illinois highway in the middle of a blizzard, and his car swerved off the road and into a snowbank. He was trapped in the snow for hours until a total stranger came to his aid and pulled his car out. The stranger asked only that he "pay it forward" one day.

Since then, Weller has done just that, rescuing thousands of people who were stranded in one way or another. Weller is otherwise known as the "San Diego Highwayman" as he was dubbed by Charles Kuralt in a CBS News story that aired in 1996. Thomas Weller is the definition of a good Samaritan. He and his vintage station wagon rescued people stranded on roadsides from 1966 until he could not continue after suffering a stroke in 2017. Fifty-one years dedicated to helping others.

His business card simply reads, "You don't owe me a thing. I've been there too. Someone once helped me out, just the way I'm helping you. If you really want to pay me back, here's what you do: don't let the chain of love end with you."

When it comes to safety, are you a giver? Do you come to the aid of others? Or are you more of a receiver. All of us, whether we've been helped by others or played the role of the Samaritan, are connected. Every time we take the time to turn in a good catch or near miss, we help others and are the Good Samaritan. The day we reach zero incidents will be because we are connected in our dedication to making injuries very rare, through the good works of those around us.

Name some recent things you have done to help someone be safe?

Is it possible to be successful in safety without the help of others?

21

MESSAGE

*"We have two ears and one mouth
so that we can listen twice as much as we speak."*
—Epictetus

*"The single biggest problem in communication
is the illusion that it has taken place."*
—George Bernard Shaw

A man signed up for a course in telepathy. After waiting to hear back for several weeks, he contacted the school, asking when the course would begin. The school said that they had been sending messages for weeks and that he had failed the course.

Did you get it? Messages are everywhere. We use many signs, warnings, and bright colors to remind us of a hazard. All signage assumes people are reading and heeding, but in our very distracted world this isn't true. Perhaps we should add a microchip that detects motion and provides a recorded verbal warning too! Sadly, that might also become something unheeded or unnoticed.

Our mindset must be one of careful monitoring of our environment for hazards. We must stay on guard. Stop. Look. Breathe. Respond.

How can we make safety warnings less likely to be ignored?

Think of a time when you missed a message. What was the result?

22

SHOES

"It's not about shoes, it's what you do in them."
—Michael Jordan

"One shoe can change your life."
—Cinderella

Perhaps my favorite movie of all time is *Forrest Gump*. The movie won six Academy Awards due to its major impact. In 2011, it was selected for preservation in the United States National Film Registry, as the Library of Congress described it as being "culturally, historically, or aesthetically significant." To me, it illustrates that we can always succeed if we believe in ourselves, but we also need someone to encourage and not give up on us when we're in doubt. Forrest's mom takes that role powerfully as she is quoted often in the film.

One of the quotes that I like the most in the movie happens in the first few minutes. Forest is telling the story of his life while sitting on a park bench talking to anyone who will listen.

FORREST:

Momma always says there's an awful lot you could tell about a person by their shoes. Where they're going. Where they've been.

The black woman stares at Forrest as he looks down at his own shoes.

(It's a foreshadowing of the story he is about to tell about his own life. His shoes are dirty.)

FORREST:

I've worn lots of shoes. I bet if I think about it real hard I could remember my first pair of shoes.

Forrest closes his eyes tightly.

FORREST:

Momma said they'd take me anywhere.

As safety leaders, our shoes are a metaphor for where we've been and where we are going. What shoes are you wearing today and what does it say about you? If they aren't "dirty" why not?

What life experience do you need to share to inspire someone to want more?

What stories can you tell?

23

DROP

You only lose what you cling to."
—Buddha

"Less is more."
—Ludwig Mies van der Rohe

The Appalachian Trail is a 2,190-mile hiking trail that extends from Georgia to Maine. At mile thirty-one of the Appalachian Trail in Georgia, there is a walk-through outfitter that offers a pack shakedown service. They help you remove from your pack all the things you don't need. A search of the internet will yield a list of the items most commonly discarded from packs.

Why mile thirty-one?

Why not save them the trouble at mile one?

Because you have to carry the load a while before you are willing to consider letting go of it. You must feel the burden before you can lay it down. In our leadership world, we are often told to do more, add this, consider this, make this part of your success formula.

Sometimes it's about subtracting something that will allow us to move forward powerfully. The next time you are stuck, think about what you might need to subtract instead of what you need to add.

When it comes to safety, do we have the courage to admit that a program, policy, or procedure is broken, ineffective, or just not being used? Instead of adding a layer (which is often proposed as a solution to safety issues), is it often about what we can subtract, so it will become simpler. Can we do simple better?

What is an example of an ineffective part of your safety efforts?

How can you reinvent this to become effective?

24

DISADVANTAGE

"Every disadvantage has its advantage."
—Johan Cruyff

*"I have all the disadvantages
required for success."*
—Larry Ellison

What do the following people have in common? Muhammad Ali, Tim Tebow, Magic Johnson, Nolan Ryan, Stephen Spielberg, Jennifer Aniston, Richard Branson, Jay Leno, Keira Knightley, Gary Cohn.

They all have what many would describe as a competitive disadvantage: dyslexia.

But all of them, and many, many more have turned dyslexia into an advantage.

With the challenges that dyslexia brings, many learn to sidestep barriers and turn what otherwise would be a disadvantage into catalysts for success. They often become good at failing without fear, and trying again and again. In time, fear of failure is diminished, and opportunity comes from trying new approaches that only occur for a dyslexic. Gary Cohn summarizes it well when he says, "I would not be where I am today without my dyslexia."

When you look at the odds being stacked against you, the challenges of your circumstances, and the unique challenges of your work environment, what "disadvantage" can you change into an advantage? If safety incidents are your disadvantage, how can you change to improve so much that you actually can say, "We would not be where we are today without the learning from our incidents."

What are some of the disadvantages in your work?

How could you change these into "competitive disadvantages"?

25

PERSEVERANCE

"Success is not the absence of failure,
it is the persistence through failure."
—Aisha Tyler

"Success is not final. Failure is not fatal.
It is the courage to continue that counts."
—Winston Churchill

Sylvia Bloom was a frugal secretary who amassed a fortune of $9 million that she bequeathed to charity.

Ronald Reed was a gas station attendant and janitor who donated $8 million to a library and hospital upon his death. Robert Morin was a librarian who accumulated wealth of $4 million that was donated.

The news is filled with stories where people of modest means amass large amounts of savings. It catches the media when the benefactors are institutions. And it surprises us. How can someone with little means amass such a fortune? It's safe to say that it was through a relentless focus on:

Perseverance: this did not happen overnight.
Discipline: staying focused and dedicated to the mission and purpose.

Happiness: By all accounts they lacked nothing, were content, and happy.

Safe: They did not take risks lightly, and made good choices.

All of these traits are connected to the way we should work both personally and professionally. We are called to be good stewards of what we've been given. Being safe requires perseverance, discipline, and, yes, even happiness. As safety leaders, we need to keep our mission and purpose in the right context. We may not get the results we want overnight, but if we persevere with discipline, the results will come.

How can we keep things in perspective when it comes to safety?

How can the power of context be used to powerfully change the way people view safety?

26

SHOW-UP

"Ninety percent of success is showing up."
—Woody Allen

*"Sometimes the bravest and most important
thing you can do is show up."*
—Brene Brown

As leaders, we must own the fact that if others are going to follow us, we must do things that make them want to follow us. I once had the benefit of walking through the woods with some of our team, looking for leaks from gas gathering lines. On one of those days, the weather was windy, rainy, and cold. I showed up at the appointed time with rain gear on, ready to go. The first question I got was, "You still want to go?" "Absolutely," was my answer. Although they were surprised at my answer, to me it was never a question.

It's on those days when we show up, those around us know that we are the real deal. I learned more that day than most days. But I also reinforced a valuable life lesson. Show up, no matter what. And there are many ways to "show up" every day: listening and observing.

Safety is the same way. We can talk all day about safety, because words are cheap. But when we "check in" with those we lead, go to the field, especially when it's not a beautiful day, we speak volumes with our actions. We earn credibility and standing. Credibility separates us from the bad advice of the world. Standing gives us a platform to influence others, transforming our words from noise to respected advice.

The challenge as safety leaders is to get out in the field and do something. Go see for yourself. Teach.

If we are asking for something different, it's our chance to show up and teach.

How much time do we spend in the field understanding the challenges of working safely?

What are ways we can earn credibility and standing?

27

UNREASONABLE

*"I was always willing to be reasonable until
I had to be unreasonable. Sometimes reasonable men
do unreasonable things."*
—Marvin Heemeyer

*"Uncomfortable doesn't mean bad,
uncomfortable simply means you're doing something
you haven't done before."*
—Michael Phelps

How many times have we said, "There must be a better way!" or "We need to find a way to…"? A relentless pursuit to improve can be initiated in many ways. We face a challenge and have a choice.

I have a quote on my office door by George Bernard Shaw, the Irish playwright, who pointed out, "The reasonable man adapts himself to the world; the unreasonable man persists in trying to adapt the world to himself. Therefore, all progress depends on the unreasonable man."

To a great extent, if we want to have a breakthrough in any topic we need to be persistently unreasonable, lest we give in and accept the status quo.

Eugene Lazowski had just finished medical school when the Nazis invaded Poland in 1939. Typhus was spreading across the country, killing an average of 750 people a day, and in an attempt to contain the disease, the Nazis increased their isolation and execution of Jews. Eugene joined the Polish Red Cross but was forbidden by the Nazis from treating Jewish patients. He did so anyway, sneaking into the Jewish ghetto under the cover of night.

One day, a Polish soldier on leave begged Eugene and his colleague to help him avoid returning to the warfront. In an attempt to help the young soldier fake a life-threatening illness, the doctors discovered that a dead strain of the Proteus OX19 bacteria in typhus would still lead to a positive test for the disease. Eugene realized that this could be used as a defense against the Nazis.

He began distributing the phony vaccine widely. Within two months, so many new (fake) cases were confirmed that Eugene successfully convinced his Nazi supervisors a typhus epidemic had broken out. In response, the Nazis began quarantining areas with suspected typhus cases, including those with Jewish inhabitants. In twelve other villages, Eugene created safe havens for Jews through these quarantines. His work deluding the Nazis would eventually save 8,000 Jewish lives.

Lives were at stake, so Eugene innovated a way to save lives. Doctors, medical researchers, and scientists all work to save lives.

Safety leaders have the same job: work to save lives by finding a way to reach as many people as possible to keep them alive.

To what lengths must we go in our pursuit of zero incidents?

What deceptions do we have about safety and how can we remove them?

28

HELP

"Men and women for others."
—Jesuit maxim, Fr. Pedro Arrupe

"Helping others is like helping yourself."
—Henry Flagler

The USS *Indianapolis* had the mission to deliver the first atomic bomb to an island in the Pacific. It did so successfully and then was given orders to proceed to the Philippines. There was no sonar escort provided, and the passage was believed to be safe. In the middle of the night, the ship was torpedoed in the bow by a Japanese sub. In the mayhem, the engine room was not able to stop the forward movement of the ship, and the ship sank in about twelve minutes.

There was very little in the way of life preservers, rafts, or provisions available as about 900 of the ship's crew of around 1,200 made it into the sea. Those who did make it, were covered in oil, burned, or injured by explosions. Then came sharks, salt poisoning, delusions, and exhaustion from treading water. The ship was not counted as overdue, due to a mistake in a handoff of personnel. So the crew spent about four and a half days in the water before being accidentally found by a bomber. What life preservers they did have were Kapok, which were fortunate to last forty-eight hours. In fact, when crew members were rescued and the life preservers cut off, they sank into the ocean. During this four-and-a-half-day ordeal, many just gave up.

Dr. Louis Haynes, the ship's doctor, who was one of the survivors, recounted how he wanted to give up many times, but then he would hear someone cry out for help. He went to them instinctively, even though he had little to offer. He said that what kept him alive was helping others. Even when recovering in the hospital after being rescued, he tried to help others when he heard them cry out.

When we start having a personal pity party about our situation, all we need to do is start helping others by sharing safety learning, providing guidance, kindness, you name it—just help others. And when we do, we too will receive a boost and that will keep us going.

If you are down about safety results (or life itself), just start helping others. Very soon, you'll bounce back because you know you are making a difference.

~

What causes us to lose motivation when it comes to safety?

Why does near miss and good catch reporting give us a mental boost?

29

SAFER

"A drop of ink may make a million think."
—George Gordon Byron

"No matter what anybody tells you, words and ideas can change the world."
—John Keating

Of all the leadership tools we have, perhaps language is the most powerful. Language is also how we shape culture and engage others.

In a study, Stanford researchers asked students to help clean up a classroom. One group was asked, "Can you help clean up?" and the other was asked, "Can you be a helper and clean up?" The second group was 33 percent more likely to help, just by adding -er to the word help.

Another study tested this with voting behavior. Group one was told, "Go vote," and Group two was told, "Be a voter." This one letter shift (adding -r) led to a 15 percent increase in voter turnout.

Why? Because we want to act in ways that confirm our identity. We all want to see ourselves as good, smart, and capable. When an action is framed as an identity, we're more likely to do it. Because now, it's who we are, not just something we do.

It also works in reverse. Cheating is bad, but being a cheater? That's much worse. Littering is bad but being a litter bug? No one wants to be that. Using nouns makes the action feel like a core part of who we are—good or bad.

So, how can we use this today? It all comes down to language.

Be a saf**er** worker, driver, parent, or friend.

Say, "Be safer."

Say, "We are safer."

Say, "We are safer drivers"

Say, "We are not safety cheaters."

Say, "I am a safer worker."

Whatever you call yourself you will become.

Why do we need to carefully choose our words?

How can you amplify these changes in your safety leadership efforts?

30

AUDACITY

"Audacity augments courage; hesitation, fear."
—Publilius Syrus

"Success is the child of audacity."
—Benjamin Disraeli

Teaching safety leadership often seems like preaching. In the context of instructing the disciples on prayer, Jesus tells a story about a midnight emergency. An unexpected guest late at night prompts a man to be hospitable and ask his neighbor for bread. Jesus said that if the neighbor did not give him food out of friendship, he would give him bread because of his "persistence" to ask in the middle of the night. But the exact word used here is not persistence.

The exact word used here is a Greek word (anaideia). It means, "without shame, impropriety, ignoring convention, shamelessness." It has often been translated "persistence," but the word really means a boldness that casts off social restraints, a shameless audacity that would lead one to bang on a neighbor's door in the middle of the night.

One of the chief complaints I have heard about safety leadership or safety professionals is that it often seems "over the top" or "too much" or isn't credible. In other words, it's too audacious. This may be true in some ungrounded instances, but it's not universally true. Have you ever thought about what it might take to wake someone up in the middle of the night? Someone who is oblivious to safety concerns may be that person who does not want to wake up. At times, if those we are leading are asleep or complacent, we have to be audacious so we can snap them out of it. Difficult times may call for difficult measures. Be bold, be lively, be energetic, and be audacious when it comes to safety.

How do personal context and life experiences influence safety?

Why do some safety efforts not reach everyone?

31

LIKE

"The problem is that real risk and perceived risk
are two different things."
—Bill Miller

"It seems to be a law of nature, inflexible and inexorable,
that those who will not risk cannot win."
—John Paul Jones

A number of years ago, I was invited to go on an offshore fishing charter for king mackerel. The weather wasn't looking good that day. If you call off a fishing charter, you usually lose your deposit. If the captain calls it off, you get your deposit back. So as we watched the looming clouds and wind, we hoped for better weather but continued on. As we left port, after passing the breakwater, the seas were about eight feet, which seemed formidable for the boat we chartered. Still, we trusted. As we continued to head out, despite our efforts to focus on the horizon, we started to feel a bit seasick. Our group then began to wonder if it was safe to continue. The group elected me to go up to the top deck and ask the captain if it was safe. So, I climbed the ladder in the heaving seas and said to the captain, "Everyone wants to know if it's safe." All the captain said in a loud gravelly voice was "I like me, nobody likes me better than me." That was it. It was up to us to connect the dots, and we did. As a misty rain hit us, the seas laid down, we had our first "fish on," and the adrenaline of the catch snapped us out of our seasick trance. We limited out by 11 AM and headed back to shore. Afterward, we asked the captain, "Where do you draw the line when it comes to bad weather?" He replied, "Right about where we were this morning."

The challenge for all of us is realizing that each of us sets our own risk levels, based on our life experiences. My risk is not your risk, and your risk is not your spouse's risk. The only way we can get on the same page about risk is to have a meaningful conversation about it before we start work. On that day, if we'd had that honest meaningful conversation, we probably would have learned more about the weather and possibly called the trip off, deposit lost or not. Sometimes the financial considerations can cause us to stay quiet when we absolutely need to speak up. Our challenge as safety leaders is to push the meaningful safety conversation.

～

Why do we hesitate to have meaningful conversations about safety?

Think of some people in different jobs who perceive risk differently from you. What drives their perception of risk?

32

INTERN

"The true test of a man's character is what he does when no one is watching."
—John Wooden

"Sometimes we are tested not to show our weaknesses but to discover our strengths."
—Tom Browning

During the early years of technology and distraction, a generation that grew up with email and texting favored these modes of communication over in-person meetings or phone calls. With prior interns and younger employees, to our dismay, we'd noticed this phenomenon and the disadvantages of electronic communication in building relationships. We had long adopted a relationship model as part of our safety support to operations. Interns need good projects but also life lessons. So, we designed a project that would fail without voice phone calls. We gave the assignment to the intern and kept quiet. As we checked for progress, we knew the electronic methods of communication would be tried and would fail. Still the answers to our questions about project status requests were vague. Finally, as the deadline for the project approached, the intern actually picked up the phone and began communicating and making progress.

When the final presentation was delivered the intern made a comment about the challenges of communicating and obtaining the information they needed, until they picked up the phone and began calling. Later we explained to the intern that the project was a test, and they had passed. The reaction was one of both relief and learning in that moment. The learning was so profound, in fact, that when the intern was hired upon graduation they asked to speak to the group of incoming interns. "Let me tell you something," she exclaimed to the group, "everything is a test!"

The same is true with safety and leadership. Everything is a test! Actions taken or not. Will you decide to lead and influence positively, or will you leave things to chance? Even when it's not convenient? Doing nothing, leaving things to chance, or trying the same techniques are not likely to be the correct answer to the test. And if you do leave things to chance, will you own it when it backfires? At the end of the day, wouldn't you rather say, "I did all I could to influence safe decisions?"

What tests have you taken in life without knowing it?

What can we do as safety leaders to change the way people view "tests"?

33

STRATEGY

*"Know your enemy and know yourself and you can fight
a hundred battles without disaster."*
—Sun Tzu

"Knowing yourself is the beginning of all wisdom."
—Aristotle

The Art of War was written by Sun Tzu in the fifth century BC. It's a military method that advocates, among a number of leadership methods, knowing yourself and your enemy. You can see this principle show up in many ways in modern life: films of opponents in football, benchmarking of competitors, news stories where we learn what other companies are doing to be successful, so we can add to our battle plan. Sun Tzu makes the point that we cannot and should not expect to be successful if we don't have a strategy, and we fully know what it will take to wage a successful war. Here are the lessons:

Lesson 1: Choose Your Battles.
Lesson 2: Timing Is Essential.
Lesson 3: Know Yourself, Know the Enemy.
Lesson 4: Have A Unique Plan.
Lesson 5: Disguise Your Plans.
Lesson 6: The Best Way to Win is Not to Fight at All.
Lesson 9: No One Profits from Prolonged Warfare.

Safety is a battle. Your safety team must develop a strategy to win the war. All you need to do is take the battle plan and execute! And remember, the key to being safe is avoiding hazards, so, as Sun Tzu says, "If he (your enemy the safety hazard) is superior in strength, evade him." If you are not ready for battle, don't fight (execute your stop work authority).

What prevents us from seeing safety leadership and performance as a battle?

In war, there is collateral damage. What is the collateral damage of safety incidents?

34

COMPLAINT

*"Be grateful for what you have and
stop complaining—it bores everybody else, does you no good,
and doesn't solve any problems."*
—Zig Ziglar

*"The pessimist complains about the wind; the optimist
expects it to change; the realist adjusts the sails."*
—William Arthur Ward

In the book *The One Minute Manager*, Ken Blanchard describes a new manager in search of advice from an "effective manager." When he finally finds the One Minute Manager, named so because it takes him a very short time to obtain results, the new manager presents his "problem." The One Minute Manager responds, "Good! That's what you've been hired to solve." The One Minute Manager tells the new manager to factually describe the problem in behavioral terms, and to also describe "what you would like to be happening in behavioral terms." The new manager did not know what he wanted. The One Minute Manager said, "If you can't tell me what you'd like to be happening, you don't have a problem yet. You're just complaining. A problem only exists if there is a difference between what is actually happening and what you desire to be happening."

As a safety leader, are you explicit with what you want to happen? If you are not, you could be seen as someone who is just complaining to everyone. Safety leaders must describe in great detail what they want in terms of safety behavior. Our challenge is to create the state of safety expectation with positive "as-desired" language in terms of the pre-job, stop work, situational awareness, effective communication, and sharing of near misses openly. Only then will you have set the bar for performance.

How do we avoid being seen as a complainer?

What is the key to setting clear safety expectations?

35

FAKE

"Be yourself, everyone else is already taken."
—Oscar Wilde

"Fake it until you become it."
—Amy Cuddy

You have probably heard the expression "fake it until you make it." Sounds hollow and inauthentic, doesn't it? What you may not realize is that we actually do have this ability, and it's very real. Dennis Prager, in his happiness video, gives this example. Suppose you are angry and in the midst of an argument with a family member and the doorbell rings. As you go to answer, in just a second you have the ability to smile and greet someone kindly, as if the argument never happened. We can choose to change our moods, and our feelings will follow our decisions.

Here's an example from my life. I once hated even the idea of running, but after being invited by a friend to run a half-marathon with him and agreeing to do so, I began to tell myself over and over that I loved it. I soon loved running! William James said that "most people never run far enough on their first wind to find out they have a second." Faking it until I made it, helped me to find that second wind and develop a love of running.

We all occasionally hit flat spots. If you ever find yourself not all-in, pumped up, excited about safety, and you are reminded that those you lead are depending on you for inspiration, you have to dig down and do your best to sincerely and authentically fake it until you make it. In that decision to answer the door with a smile on your face, you will eventually develop a true passion and love of all things safety.

What damage can inauthentic safety efforts cause?

Do people sense when we are not being authentic?

36

MISSION

"Your mission should you choose to accept it..."
—*Mission Impossible* recording.

*"The two most important days in your life are the day
you are born and the day you find out why."*
—Mark Twain

Guy Whidden was a paratrooper machine gunner who was part of the famous Airborne 101 operation as part of the Normandy invasion on D-Day. He was twenty years old at the time, and as the drop time came, he was anxious to leave the plane. The drop was from a very low altitude, around 300 feet, so the paratroopers knew they would hit the ground hard, and for some, the parachutes did not open properly. Planes were crashing, tracer bullets were flying everywhere, anti-aircraft fire was present, and Whidden likened it to the 4th of July, with lots of noise. As he descended, a mortar round exploded and he felt something hit his chest. As he went to inspect the damage later, he found that his prayer book, *Rations—100 Days*, had stopped the shrapnel from hitting him. He called it divine intervention.

For anyone who has had an experience of divine intervention like this, we likely ask ourselves, "Why me?" And to this there can only be one answer (obtained from Hillel the Elder):

If not you, who? And if not now, when? Like Whidden, you made it because you are on a mission, a life mission. Whidden went on to tell this story and many others like it as part of his life mission which finally ended with his passing at the age of ninety-nine in September of 2022.

For every close call, there is a mission to fulfill, and a choice to make it a personal mission. And that is exactly what we need to do with safety, make it personal, make it our own mission! As leaders, the challenge is to ACCEPT this mission and embrace it as we live life to the fullest, witnessing to the small miracles and affirmations to as many as we can.

What prevents us from seeing that our lives are really a mission?

How can we fulfill the mission of keeping others safe through our experiences?

37

INVEST

*"My wealth has come from a combination of living
in America, some lucky genes, and compound interest."*
—Warren Buffet

*"Compound interest is proof that you
can get rich slowly."*
—Dave Ramsey

It is believed that Albert Einstein once quipped that the most powerful force in the universe is the principle of compounding. Very simply, compound interest means that you begin to earn interest on the interest you receive, which multiplies your money at an accelerated rate.

If you have $500 and earn 10 percent interest per year, you will have $550 after one year. Then, if you earn 10 percent interest the next year on that $550, you end up with $605 by the end of year two. The process continues until, eventually, your original $500 may be eclipsed by the amount of interest you gained.

If you don't invest the $500 in an account with 10 percent annual interest, you'll lose the opportunity to earn $50 or more per year in interest. In ten years, your $500 could be $1,296.87. But if you don't invest it, it'll still be $500 ten years later.

Opportunity cost is the amount of potential gain an investor misses out on when they commit to one investment choice over another.

Safety is cumulative. There are no light switches that can be magically turned on and all our safety challenges are then solved. The choice to invest in safety through advocacy or not is exactly like compound interest. Another example of opportunity cost is something as simple as choosing between advocating safety or not advocating safety. What are you losing out on if you choose one over the other? Intangible but definitely an opportunity! Opportunity cost doesn't always need to apply to investments or money; it can also apply to life decisions.

⁓

Make a list of the investments you have made in safety?

How long do we need to wait for a safety investment to pay off?

38

INTEGRITY

"If you have integrity, nothing else matters. If you don't have integrity, nothing else matters."
—Alan K. Simpson

"Honesty is the first chapter in the book of wisdom."
—Thomas Jefferson

Captain Sully Sullenberger, the pilot who landed on the Hudson River after his plane had a bird strike that stopped both engines, recounted that day in a Parade magazine article published in 2009. Sullenberger described, "What I Got Back."

> *All of my clothing came back in good condition and with that strong fabric-softener smell. I was also glad to get back my Jeppesen airway manual, which contains the charts for all of the airports we serve. Still taped neatly inside, weathered but readable, was the fortune from a fortune cookie that I'd gotten at a Chinese restaurant in San Mateo, Calif., sometime in the late 1980s.*
>
> *It read: "A delay is better than a disaster."*
>
> *I thought that was good advice at the time, and so I'd kept it in the manual ever since.*

That fortune reminded me of an unexpected question my daughter Kate asked me when she was 9. I was driving her to school, and out of the blue, she asked me: "Daddy, what does integrity mean?"

After thinking about it, I came up with what, in retrospect, was a pretty good answer: " Integrity means doing the right thing even when it's not convenient."

Integrity is the core of my profession. An airline pilot has to do the right thing every time, even if that means delaying or canceling a flight to address a maintenance or other issue, even if it means inconveniencing 183 people who want to get home, including the pilot. By delaying a flight, I am ensuring that they will get home."

As safety leaders, all we have is integrity.

How does walking the talk matter in how we influence and lead?

How can we use integrity to build a strong foundation to our safety efforts?

39

COMMUNICATE

*"The most important thing in communication is
to hear what isn't being said."*
—Peter Drucker

*"The way we communicate with others and ourselves
ultimately determines the quality of our lives."*
—Tony Robbins

In the movie *Cool Hand Luke*, Strother Martin, after dealing with the repeated defiance of Paul Newman, gives a famous speech in which he says, "What we have here is a failure to communicate." In any organization, there are many breakdowns and lost opportunities that are related to a failure to communicate. Our messages are either lost in translation, like a game of "telephone" or even no communication at all can cause failure.

I did some research. It turns out that many air disasters have been caused by a failure to communicate, and sometimes getting just one word wrong caused a crash. Wars have started by failure to communicate well. The Piper Alpha tragedy was caused by a failure to communicate. The Deep Water Horizon disaster was, at its core, a failure to communicate. Ikea picture-only instructions are likely a failure to communicate and potentially responsible for two deaths when dressers toppled over and killed toddlers.

All of us have witnessed failures to communicate firsthand. It happens every day. But we also witness communication success every day. Think about the last time you provided a credit card or confirmation number over the phone. Chances are the recipient will read it back to you to confirm accuracy. If we don't pass along a safety warning or advisory, or get the communication right, can the same be true? We need to use the read-back technique—what did you hear?" Coach those you lead to confirm by saying, "What I heard was…" Imagine your safety messages are critical to get right. Verify receipt.

What good are safety leadership moments if they are not shared?

Describe your personal commitment to sharing safety knowledge.

40

QUIET

"Silence is the sleep that nourishes wisdom."
—Francis Bacon

*"The quieter you become,
the more you are able to hear."*
—Rumi

In 1979, Jim Kitchen, Bill Wagner, and Travis Miller attended Sul Ross State University in Alpine, Texas. They wanted a quiet place to study with a great view. So, they hauled a desk and chair up Hancock Hill, which overlooks the Big Bend (a vast curve of the Rio Grande in remote southwest Texas). The view there is incredible. Sometime after, one of the three decided to leave a notebook with a message in the top drawer of the desk just to see what might happen. Visitors to the desk continued leaving messages. Over the last forty years, the notebooks filled with the thoughts of visitors have been archived in the university library. The notes range from humorous to heartfelt, but all represent a moment taken to gain clarity of thought and reach the heart and mind. Today it's a bit of a tourist attraction.

All of us need time to gain clarity of thought, separating the busyness of our days from the real priorities of our lives. Nature is a powerful way to help us get in touch with what is truly important. Many of us work outdoors, but even so, the beauty of creation that surrounds us can be lost. Just a quick walk outside in the middle of our day can reset our minds and provide clarity.

The same is true for safety. Most safety incidents occur when our mind is elsewhere. We can benefit from stopping and reflecting on what would make a successful safe day, safe project, or safe task. As the old Coke slogan said, "It's the pause that refreshes." A safer mindset does not happen automatically. We must be deliberate in the work of maintaining focus on the task at hand. As safety leaders, we must promote this practice so that all whom we influence truly know they can and they must take some time out to be quiet and safer.

What is preventing you from setting up a daily calendar block or reminder to stop, breathe, and get in touch with your true priorities?

How does an effective STOP program relate to taking time to gather our thoughts?

41

DETERMINATION

"Energy and persistence conquer all things."
—Ben Franklin

*"Strength does not come from physical capacity.
It comes from an indomitable will."*
—Mahatma Gandhi

Hawaii was discovered around AD 1000—no one knows the exact date—by a group of seafaring Polynesians who inhabited and explored many of the islands in the South Pacific. If you look at a map of the world, you'll notice that Hawaii is one of the most isolated spots on the planet. It's already incredible that it was discovered so early in human history. But what they did to arrive there makes the story even more amazing. Because of its isolation, they would never have known Hawaii was even there.

They suspected it was there though. They noticed a bird called the Golden Plover which migrated north out into the open water every year. Land must have been out there somewhere—they just couldn't see it.

So, they set sail from the Marquesas Islands to follow them. That island is as close as you can get to Hawaii, but it's still about 2,500 miles away. Nowadays, it takes roughly thirty days to sail to Hawaii from Marquesas using modern-day equipment. Back then, they were only using carved wooden boats and their own understanding of naval navigation. The Polynesians followed the birds closely, but they always flew faster than they could paddle. They could only keep up with them for short distances. At some point, they would lose track and have to turn back.

Each year they would try again, picking up where they left off the previous year. Years passed by and they kept getting farther into the Pacific. But still they never saw land. It took the Polynesians 400 years to finally reach Hawaii using this method. Four hundred years!

And it's the same with safety. Getting to zero takes determination and trying over and over. We have a sense of urgency, and we are looking for results much sooner than 400 years. Like the Polynesians, we know that zero is there! We see the signs and clues of success like the Polynesians saw the plover, and we are following the safety plover. Can you imagine the failed attempts to keep up with the plovers? As each expedition came back, if they made it back, how were they welcomed? Likely with encouragement! But also with some naysayers who turned out to be wrong! They just kept learning, until they made it. Our challenge is to maintain hope and keep our eyes on the signs of zero.

What does it take to not lose heart in attaining zero incidents?

How can we keep our eyes on the prize of safety?

42

JOY

"Don't be ashamed to need help. Like a soldier storming a wall, you have a mission to accomplish. And if you've been wounded and you need a comrade to pull you up? So what?"
—Marcus Aurelius

"The only mistake you can make is not asking for help."
—Sandeep Jauhar

Alice was an elderly neighbor who lived alone. Her husband had passed, and her children lived far away. We made a full decision to "adopt" her. She would call occasionally asking for help with household issues like her garage door or her internet service. After helping her, I would always say, "You know, Alice, you can call me anytime for anything." She would usually say, "I know… but you are busy." One day, after helping Alice, prompted by a holy nudge I questioned.

"Alice, do you know the feeling you get when you volunteer at church?"

"Yes," she replied, "I feel wonderful." So, I asked her, "Alice, why would you deprive me of my joy?"

The question for leaders is, "Why do we deprive others of the joy of helping?"

The biggest challenge that new leaders face is realizing that they cannot do it all themselves.

I once heard an expression from my team, but I did not fully appreciate it. I'd say, "Thanks for helping," and the response was often, "We just help." But later, as I heard this again and again, I realized that there is a bold, underlined, italicized word in that sentence. *Just.* Which means we don't go backwards, and we don't focus on unproductive energy. We just know that someone needs help, and we just help because that is enough. No further explanation is required.

To be effective safety leaders, we are required to allow others to help us. That help comes in the form of better, safer methods to do our work. We learn this from Good Catches, Near Misses and the meaningful conversations about avoiding hazards that naturally follow.

It's like nothing else. It gives us great pleasure and happiness. Pure joy really.

Do you want that joy? Turn in a good catch.

Believe that doing so will be just like helping out at church or helping your neighbor. Because it really is the same.

What are the barriers to asking for help?

How do we discourage others from asking for help?

43

LANGUAGE

"The limits of my language mean the limits of my world."
—Ludwig Wittgenstein

"Language exerts hidden power, like the moon on the tides."
—H. R. B. Smith

Vaughn Smith of Gaithersburg, Maryland, is a carpet cleaner. But his real gift is language. Vaughn is a hyperpolyglot, which is defined as someone who can speak at least eleven languages. He dreams in ten languages, and Vaughn has learned about forty languages. He has never taken language classes and is self-taught. Although never diagnosed, he and his mother believe that he is probably autistic.

Vaughn believes that his gift of language is not to attract attention or for monetary gain. He says, "Language is a key to someone's culture, to someone's world." Whether it's watching a client's face light up when he speaks to them in their native tongue or showing Indigenous children in rural Mexico that their language is valuable and worth preserving, Vaughn views his gifts as a way of connecting with other people.

Vaughn has noticed that when you make the effort to speak to someone in their native language, they are grateful, and relationships often follow.

Are we speaking the language of safety? Are we fluent in the native safety language of our team? Maybe we've never taught ourselves the language.

What words would you want to hear from your supervisor to be grateful that they were making the effort to speak in your native language of safety? Write those words down. Then speak those words often to those you influence.

Struggling with what to say? If it was me, I'd want to hear something like: "I care about you. Your safety is important to me. Please don't take any chances today. I need you to get things right and make a safe day. I expect you to get things right because I'm counting on you."

What is preventing us from speaking the native language of safety?

How can we teach ourselves the right words?

44

MEANING

"Words mean more than what is set down on paper. It takes the human voice to infuse them with deeper meaning."
—Maya Angelou.

"And it is very difficult to have a meaningful life without meaningful work."
—Jim Collins

Viktor Frankl survived the Nazi concentration camps, having spent time in the notorious Auschwitz camp. When he made it out of Auschwitz, he then wrote one of the most powerful books ever written in our times: *Man's Search for Meaning.* What Frankl summarized in his book is still quite relevant today. Frankl's main idea was, "He who has a why to live can bear almost any how." He said, "In the Nazi concentration camps, one could have witnessed that those who knew there was a task waiting for them to fulfill were more apt to survive." This idea reshapes how we think about suffering, success, and what it means to truly live. Frankl wasn't just a survivor, he was a psychiatrist who introduced an idea that was quite radical during those times, and he was professionally ostracized as a result. His ideas are:

- We're not driven by pleasure.
- We're not driven by power.
- We're driven by meaning.

He called it "logotherapy," the belief that our deepest motivation is to find purpose in life. Here is one idea that Frankl put forward that is very relevant to our times: Burnout isn't about doing too much—it's about doing too little of what matters. We don't break from effort. We break from emptiness.

Frankl said that meaning shows up in three places:

- What you create
- Who you love
- How you grow through suffering

We can't always change our circumstances, but we can always choose our response, and in that choice, we have great power. We don't need to find meaning in everything, we just need something that makes it all worth it. We just need a reason to get up, a reason to keep going, in a world that seems to be obsessed with speed, status, and success. Frankl's work reminds us that the most important thing isn't how you're living, it's why.

When it comes to safety, meaning is central to our motivation to work safely. We think about our "what matters most" as the main thing. As leaders we need to relate to our "what matters most" when we influence others to work safely and remind everyone to keep our "what matters most," in the front of our minds.

—

Name some ways to infuse meaning into our safety efforts

How do we grow through the suffering of safety incidents?

45

IMAGINATION

"Imagination is more important than knowledge. For knowledge is limited, whereas imagination embraces the entire world, stimulating progress, giving birth to evolution."
—Albert Einstein

"Come with me and you'll be in a world of pure imagination."
—Gene Wilder in *Willy Wonka and The Chocolate Factory.*

In the 1960s, George Land was hired by NASA to administer a test that could identify the creative potential of engineers and scientists. *The Creative Thinking Assessment* measured divergent thinking, or the ability to imagine multiple solutions to a problem.

Land did a study on 1,600 children from ages three to five and found 98 percent scored as "genius" level for creative thinking. The test presented children with problems and asked them to come up with new or different ideas to solve them. As the children aged, their scores plummeted. By age ten, only 30 percent scored at the genius level, and by age fifteen, the genius level dropped to 12 percent. When adults were tested, only 2 percent retained a high-level of creativity. Land believed that our traditional education system, and our emphasis on memorization, standardization, and conformity were largely responsible for this decline. Schools, he argued, were suppressing creative thinking by encouraging students to follow prede-termined paths rather than exploring their own ideas. Land concluded that non-creative thinking was learned.

Imagination is a critical skill in being safe. Creativity enables us to anticipate potential hazards and develop creative solutions to unforeseen problems. Imagination helps prevent complacency, *which is a failure to adequately consider potential hazards*, because we rely on our imagination to create a "what if" and "what could go wrong" mindset so we can find ways to mitigate those possible hazards. If it strains our imagination to think in a creative way, it could be because our creative-ness has been driven out of us, and we just need to find ways to strengthen our imagination. This can be accomplished with a very fulsome and creative "Pre-Job Hazard Identification" process. We must all create new positive habits of being creative about what could go wrong if we expect to stay safe.

~

What role does imagination plan in our long-term safety vision and strategy?

How can we practice being more imaginative?

46

ASKING

"Life's not about how hard of a hit you can give... it's about how many you can take and still keep moving forward."
—Sylvester Stallone

"Every morning we are born again. What we do today is what matters most."
—Buddha

He often hid in the bedroom while his parents threw abusive language at each other. When they finally ended their marriage, he passed between foster homes and was expelled from fourteen schools by the age of thirteen. He ended up in a high school for troubled youth. Nobody believed the kid from the broken home would make it.

His dreams persisted. He was going to be an actor, writer, and director in Hollywood! His good looks helped him land some minor roles. He took any job, cleaning lion cages at Central Park Zoo, ushering at a movie house, and anything he could do to pay the rent, but also wound up living in a bus terminal for three weeks.

By 1975, he had $106 in the bank, his wife was pregnant, and he couldn't pay the rent on his run-down apartment. After selling his dog for $50, he wrote a screenplay in about twenty hours about a loser like himself. When he shopped his script around Hollywood, the wannabe screenwriter was rejected a total of fifteen hundred times. But he got up after each knock-down to try another round with the media moguls. He did receive some offers to buy the script for as much as $360K but declined because they wouldn't let him star in it. It was all or nothing. Finally, United Artists took a chance and limited the risk by making it low budget. He could star in his own film.

His budget of $1 million forced him to finish filming the movie in twenty-eight days. It started out with mixed reviews and small audiences. Soon, Sylvester Stallone's *Rocky* went to the top in 1976. Those that rejected him were shocked when it became one of the biggest blockbusters of all time—grossing more than $100 million. There was even more shock when *Rocky* won the Academy Award for Best Picture in 1977.

The rest is history. Rocky and its many sequels are one of the most successful movie franchises of all time. Sylvester Stallone is one of the biggest action stars in movie history. It all started with a relentless ***asking*** for an opportunity.

Why does the Rocky story attract us? Because the "hero's journey" that Sylvester Stallone and his *Rocky* took is really ours too. All of us must fall before we can rise to become heroes.

When it comes to safety, like Stallone, we must keep *asking*, 1,500 times if necessary, "How can we improve?" until we have attained zero incidents. Leaders ask questions and never stop listening. If we can get up, the fight isn't over.

Why do safety initiatives die?

How can we be sure that our safety efforts won't be knocked down and stay down?

47

GRATEFUL

*"The more you practice the art of thankfulness,
the more you have to be thankful for."*
—Norman Vincent Peale

*"If the only prayer you ever say in your entire life
is thank you, it will be enough."*
—Meister Eckhart

On an elevator in downtown Houston, everyone was headed to work. There was no shortage of glum faces. I announced to everyone, "You know we don't have to do this." One person, with a puzzled look, retorted, "Oh yeah?" I said, "We get to do this, we get to work, there is a difference." Extensive, conclusive research has shown that if you express gratitude on a regular basis, you'll be happy, you'll be more creative, you'll be more fulfilled—you might even live ten years longer.

And you'll be safer too!

Have you ever reflected on what it takes to even be able to work safe? If you take a world view, first we must live in a country where safe work is an expectation and a right. We would also need a company that genuinely cares, and coworkers that care. Perhaps, most importantly, we would need a place where camaraderie exists that builds a strong foundation. We need to be grateful for all of this.

During Thanksgiving, it's important to think about what makes it possible to work safe. Historically, we've seen working conditions and expectations that were impossible, but we have everything we need. Knowledge has come at the expense of the injured. Leaders make sure we don't waste the knowledge! Make sure you create an environment of learning.

Psychologist Robert Emmons has devoted much of his life's work to the study of gratitude and the role it plays in our happiness. Here are just a few of the many proven health benefits of gratitude:

Physical: 1) Stronger immune systems; 2) Less bothered by aches and pains; 3) Lower blood pressure; 4) Exercise more and take better care of their health; 5) Sleep longer and feel more refreshed upon waking.

Psychological: 1) Higher levels of positive emotions; 2) More alert, alive, and awake; 3) More joy and pleasure; 4) More optimism and happiness.

Social: 1) More helpful, generous, and compassionate; 2) More forgiving; 3) More outgoing; 4) Feel less lonely and isolated.

How do you gain gratitude and the host of benefits that come with it? Gratitude journals are a good way, or each evening at a meal everyone names three things that happened that day they are grateful for. It can be as simple as a laugh, a situation, or some food you enjoyed.

How does gratitude connect to being able to focus on our work?

What are your safety gratitudes?

48

LISTENING

"A wise man speaks because he has something to say;
a fool speaks because he has to say something."
—Plato

"When people talk, listen completely.
Most people never listen."
—Ernest Hemingway

As leaders, we use our words to shape outcomes. In a world where our attention span is being constantly challenged, leaders need effective language to communicate well. Our mission is to find ways to reach everyone that we influence in a compelling way. First, we have to gain the attention of our audience.

George Lucas had this same challenge when the character Yoda was being created for Star Wars.

"Yoda had a very distinctive way of talking, and it was done purposely because if you were speaking regular English, people don't listen that much, but if he has an accent, or it's really hard to understand what he's saying, they focus on what he's saying. He was basically the philosopher of the movie, so he was talking about all of the things in long talking scenes and stuff where I had to figure out a way to get people to actually listen, especially twelve-year-olds."

We especially recall these Yoda quotes: "Try not. Do or do not. There is no try", "The greatest teacher, failure is", and "Much to learn, you still have."

As safety leaders, we must craft our message in a way that our audience will actually listen. This is one of the most difficult challenges. We could reverse our sentence structure like Yoda did, but there are more ways to speak effectively so others will listen. One technique is to slow our rate of speech down and use the fewest words possible. George Lucas planned this, and we need to plan it too.

Why does the tone and speed of our safety messaging matter?

What changes do we need to make to our speech patterns to improve listening?

49

WORKAROUND

*"When you have exhausted all possibilities,
remember this: you haven't."*
—Thomas Edison

*"When you first start trying to solve a problem,
the first solutions you come up with are very complex,
and most people stop there. But if you keep going and live
with the problem and peel more layers of the onion off, you can
often arrive at some very elegant and simple solutions."*
—Steve Jobs

There were eleven of us for dinner every night (our parents, seven kids, and our grandparents). Imagine the chore of preparing enough food for everyone. Now imagine the challenge of preparing food that everyone liked. My mom was an adventurous cook, trying out new foods and recipes from around the world on all of us and encouraging us to try things we had never tasted. A spinach salad was described as "French lettuce." It exposed us to new cuisines, made dinner fun, and gave us something to talk about. If anyone was ever so bold as to turn their nose up at what was served, there was always peanut butter and jelly, which was offered self-serve. Perhaps the offer should have also been made so that the person who did not like what was being served would prepare everything the next evening.

In business, I've witnessed something similar happen. Someone does not like what is being served, so they make themselves a workaround (equivalent to the PB&J sandwich) to get the job done. It's not that there is anything wrong with what is being served (workflows, processes, safe work procedures, paperwork, slight inconvenience), it's just that they decide that they don't like it. And perhaps they have not even tried the "French lettuce."

Workarounds are part of every business and usually develop when a process, procedure, or workflow is misunderstood, broken, inefficient, or outdated. When safety workarounds occur, there could be new risks that have not been properly vetted. The workarounds can become elaborate. The real answer is to stop and talk about the issue and fix the process (the equivalent to making tomorrow's meal).

As safety leaders when we see workarounds, we need to always stop, listen, evaluate, and focus on fixing the long-term underlying issues. Only then will we be transformative in our leadership.

~

Name some workarounds in your current business. How can these workarounds destroy value, efficiency and safety?

Can you think of a time when a workaround caused an incident?

50

TRUTH

"If you tell the truth, you don't have to remember anything."
— Mark Twain

*"Integrity is doing the right thing, even when
no one is watching."*
—C.S. Lewis

Greg grew up in the outback of California. He had trouble staying still and focusing in school (what we now know is ADHD), so he poured himself into an active outdoor life, including cycling. At fifteen, he was competing at a high level. He later said that his "triumph over the symptoms was found atop two thin tires over many dusty miles." He continued to be successful and, in 1986, won the 2,200-mile Tour de France. Later that year, while hunting for turkey, he was accidentally shot and nearly died. Doctors worked to remove as many pellets as possible from his critical organs but could not remove them all, including two in his heart lining. The lead from the pellets would impact his health for many years without hope for a remedy. Still, Greg began working to return to cycling, and amazingly, he again won the Tour de France in 1989 and again in 1990. Greg had reached the top of cycling.

Soon, Lance Armstrong became the new star by winning seven Tour de France titles. But Greg knew Lance was a cheater because he was associating with a doctor known for performance-enhancing techniques. Greg could have stayed quiet, but instead he spoke out about Lance and lost financially due to the impacts on his cycling business and endorsements. He was dismissed by the cycling world as an envious troublemaker.

We now have the facts. Greg LeMond was telling the truth and Lance Armstrong was lying. Greg is now recognized for his truth. His story tells us that integrity always matters, and we cannot ever compromise on truth. When it comes to safety, indeed integrity is all we have. It's the right way or not at all.

Name a time when bending a safety rule could have damaged integrity and your credibility.

Give some examples of actions that damage integrity.

51

UNIQUE

"Strength lies in differences, not similarities."
—Stephen Covey

"Differences allow us to be fascinated with each other."
—Tom Robbins

When snowflakes fall from the sky, along the route, they pass through some different environments, temperatures, humidity, speed, and turbulence, all of which shapes how the snowflake appears once it reaches the ground. Wilson Bentley, a farmer in Vermont, was called "The Snowflake Man" because at the age of nineteen he became the first to photograph a single ice crystal. He made a flexible bellows contraption from the microscope he had been given at the age of fifteen. He photographed over 5,000 snowflakes in his lifetime and in his later years remarked that he had never seen two snowflakes alike, and so the story that we all heard began: no two snowflakes were exactly alike. In 1988, about 100 years after Wilson Bentley's first photograph, scientist Nancy Knight at the National Center for Atmospheric Research was studying high-altitude cirrus clouds, and she collected and found two identical "baby" snowflakes early in their journey toward the ground.

Like baby snowflakes, we all start out about the same, but our many life experiences shape us, just like the snowflakes, and the result is that we are beautifully different. At this time of Christmas and the holidays, as we count our blessings, we can appreciate that what makes us strong is our collective life experiences. In the same way, with safety each of our perspectives is both a strength and an experience that is a teachable moment for others that must be shared.

As leaders, we also recognize that we must make efforts to reach everyone where they are and help them to lead from exactly where their boots are.

Have a very blessed and safe Christmas, holidays, and New Year!

How can you harness the power of our differences in your safety efforts?

Why do we need different life experiences to produce a better result?

52

REMEMBER

*"Those who cannot remember the past
are condemned to repeat it."*
—George Santayana

"People remember how you made them feel."
—Maya Angelou

"Auld Lang Syne" is a Scottish poem that became a customary song for New Year's and other important times. The Scottish "Auld Lang Syne" translates to "Long long ago." But it's not just a drinking song for midnight at New Year's. There is much more meaning. It's a call to remember longstanding friendships and to not forget old times.

And so it is with being safer. So much of our efforts are focused on learning from past close calls and incidents. We work tirelessly to keep these things "front of brain" so we don't repeat them. Think about how many procedures, processes, and administrative controls were born from past incidents. We have many to thank for our current safety knowledge, and we should not forget them. And longstanding friendships? Our work friendships will sustain us in the cause to be safe for what matters most.

I once asked a large audience to write down a safety story and what they learned. I collected the stories and made a booklet and passed it out to everyone. That little booklet could have been titled *Remember*.

As you toast the old year and ring in the new, don't forget! Remember what you've learned and use this knowledge to stay safe.

What are some of the greatest safety lessons you've ever learned?

How can you use the collective safety lessons around those who you work with to teach and motivate?

53

LAGNIAPPE

"There are no traffic jams on the extra mile."
—Zig Ziglar

*"The difference between ordinary and extraordinary
is that little extra."*
—Jimmy Johnson

Growing up in South Louisiana, I became familiar with the word "lagniappe" (pronounced LAN-yap). It originates from the Spanish and Quechua word *yapa* (from the Incans) and *la napa*, meaning a little something extra or a small gift given by a merchant to a customer in addition to a purchase. There are some classic examples that you are likely familiar with, like a baker's dozen, where you buy twelve items and get thirteen. This old custom is still widely practiced in Louisiana. Mark Twain said it was "a word worth travelling to New Orleans to get." I witnessed this growing up, when a grocer would give something special to a regular customer, or an order of fries would be added to my lunch. It's a cultural thing that builds a relationship with a merchant. Aren't you more likely to frequent a business that shows gratitude?

In safety, we have this same opportunity to bless someone and show gratitude with something extra. It's usually our knowledge, experience, and dedication. There are fifty-two weeks in the year, and this book has more than fifty-two passages. Why? Lagniappe! You have the same opportunity to give something extra to your safety leadership.

In your leadership are you giving the minimum, or are you generous? Which would you rather it be?

What do you want your safety legacy to be?

54

CARING

"Love begins by taking care of the closest ones—
the ones at home."
—Mother Teresa

"The simple act of caring is heroic."
—Edward Albert

I had many years in the safety field, seeking the best methods. Every now and then, you come across something so profound that you never forget it.

This happened to me when teaching the Safety Leadership Seminars at ConocoPhillips. We did an exercise where we asked everyone in the class:

"What is the most important quality of a leader and therefore a safety leader?"

Everyone would suggest the most important qualities of a leader. To be fair, we received many good answers, plenty of great qualities, and we wrote them down on the display. Rarely we got the word we were looking for. We got many answers. The one we were looking for was "caring!" We gave a new definition.

A safety leader is "a person who CARES enough to take the action to keep THEMSELVES & OTHERS free from danger or injury through guidance, persuasion, direction, and/or setting the example."

When setting priorities for safety, there can be no higher priority than making it abundantly clear that you care about people.

Why is caring the most important attribute of a safety leader?

How does caring relate to gaining standing, or the ability to be taken seriously?

55

OWNERSHIP

"When you think everything is someone's fault, you will suffer a lot. When you realize that everything springs only from yourself, you will learn both peace and joy."
—Dalai Lama

"Until you take ownership for your life, you will always be chasing happiness."
—Sean Stephenson

In their book *Extreme Ownership*, Jocko Willink and Leif Babin present a series of battlefield stories, and how the idea of extreme ownership relates to leadership and winning. In one chapter, a story is told about Navy Seal "hell week." One boat crew consistently came in last, crew six, and crew two came in first consistently. Eventually the instructor made a change between boat crew two and boat crew six. He just swapped the leader. What happened?

Boat crew six won, but boat crew two stayed competitive. Why?

It was because the boat crew two leader was an encourager, the crew "owned it," and the encouragement was contagious enough to stay with the crew when their leader was replaced. This supports the adage: if you believe in it, you will achieve it.

Safety leaders can wear many leadership hats, but perhaps the winning hat is to be an encourager. When morale is down, the positive support of an encourager can be what it takes to make a comeback. When times are tough, rowing the boat can seem impossible, but the encourager will be the force that keeps people rowing, causing them to accept ownership. Even if that safety leader leaves, the positive influence of taking ownership will last.

What leadership actions are discouraging?

Describe how taking ownership is the key to safety success.

EPILOGUE

When interviewing someone for a role, we often put this topic out for conversation:

"All of us learn things in our careers, some technical, some non-technical. The non-technical things often rise to 'life lessons.' Have you had any life lessons you've picked up along the way? If you have, please tell us about them."

We ask this question to raise the topic of learning. We want people who will be like a sponge and soak up knowledge from everywhere. If they can't describe these life lessons, we think carefully about whether they will fit in.

If we can tell some of these stories, it demonstrates that we are life-long learners. The purpose of this book is to share some of the many life lessons I've picked up along the way.

We hope and pray that this book has been a blessing to you. If it has, we'd love to hear from you. We can be reached on LinkedIn or at paul@inspiritusproperties.com.

If you enjoyed these leadership moments, please look for Volume 2.

INDEX OF TOPICS